APPLIED EMOTIONAL INTELLIGENCE

Learn how to master your feelings, motivate yourself and lead others to achieve goals and have the right social interactions.

BY

DEREK GONEKE

CONTENTS

INTRODUCTION

The original theory of emotional intelligence was developed by two US psychologists. Peter Salovey and John Mayer in 1990 defined this as a learned ability to perceive, understand and express our feelings accurately and to control our emotions so that they work for us, not against us.

In other words, no matter whose definition you use, EI is about: Knowing how you and others feel and what to do about it. Knowing what feels good and what feels bad and how to get from bad to good

Possessing emotional awareness, sensitivity, and skills that will help us to stay positive and maximize our long-term happiness and well-being.

Emotionally intelligent people can manage their emotions, and not let their emotions get the better of them. If they become angry or upset, they don't take their emotions out on others; rather, they deal with the issue calmly and find a way to control and mitigate their anger.

Emotion and intelligence are two terms that are combined more as time passes. Many people have an innate ability to utilize the strengths of human nature to further success. Individuals with a high level of emotional intelligence have an insightful understanding of themselves and others. If a situation invokes stress, the person with a high level of emotional intelligence has an instinctive ability to console and comfort.

Individuals with high levels of emotional intelligence can easily empathize with others. They see the situation from another perspective without stress. While some people are born with abnormally high levels of emotional intelligence, it is a trait that the majority of people can learn. There is a myriad of benefits to EI encouragement. Individuals with high emotional intelligence are noted to achieve better results in projects. They can develop greater professional networks and achieve higher productivity.

Experts today cite many benefits to having a high level of EI. EI is usually measured by using four different areas of ability. The first level is that of general perception. What emotions are others feeling? People with strong EI can detect the presence of emotion in themselves and others. They can often spot minor emotional problems that might lead to serious issues in the future.

The next area of measurement is that of using emotions. High EI often indicates a uni☐ue ability for problem-solving and decision making. These cognitive traits are beneficial in the work environment. Experts have stated that emotional intelligence is the most important form of intelligence in the workplace. It is a natural process of motivation and problem management.

The third area of measurement in emotional intelligence is that of just understanding emotions. Human communication involves many forms of non-verbal language. People with high EI are capable of reading this emotional language in others. They are not intimidated by complicated relationships and can easily mediate disagreements. High EI individuals can coach positive emotions in co-workers and associates. They are wonderful motivators with genuine and sincere enthusiasm. They are agile at goal setting and can direct a group towards achievable and rewarding project conclusions.

The final area of testing for EI is that of managing emotions. This is the ability to bring out the most positive and constructive emotions in everyone. Those with the ability to manage emotions can often overlook their negative feelings and maintain focus on goals and the necessary positive emotions to achieve them. EI-oriented individuals can gauge their own reactions and behaviors. This helps them see what influences their behaviors have on others before acting.

Emotional intelligence is a practical necessity in any office setting. The intensive self-reflection involved opens communication with others. High EI individuals can achieve much more through self-awareness of goals and limitations. Because so many professions involve team atmospheres, emotional intelligence is a productive and beneficial element in the workplace.

People with high EI are frequent motivators. They are capable of understanding their moods and drives. They are equally capable of understanding the same qualities in others. They can urge fellow employees or teammates to strive for the best work possible. A person with high emotional intelligence has a strong ability to control or change negative feelings. They naturally think before behaving on an impulse.

Entrepreneurs/Leaders are frequently gifted with a strong amount of EI. They have a zeal for their work that goes beyond money or status. This helps them realistically judge themselves and successfully interact with clients. EI allows an individual to break down major achievements into simple steps. This goal setting can have a positive impact on any developing industry.

General technical or mechanical intelligence will remain a valued trait in the business world. It is not the only strength examined today. A high level of emotional intelligence can improve the work experience and the workplace.

EMOTIONAL INTELLIGENCE: THE KEY TO SUCCESS?

If you've done any professional networking at all, you've probably heard this line: "People like to do business with those they like and trust." I believe this is true, and I also feel that those who succeed in the business world typically have qualities that transcend competence or intelligence.

This doesn't mean being inept or not very smart will get you far, but it does demonstrate the importance of emotional intelligence as a precursor of success. What is emotional intelligence? It's the ability to effectively use self-awareness and appropriate social skills to build consensus, manage people toward a common goal and in essence, be "liked"; it's the X factor that can make an intangible difference for entrepreneurs or those seeking to climb the corporate ladder.

You're probably familiar with intelligence quotient (IQ), a measure of brainpower that changes very little after your teens. What you may not be aware of is your emotional quotient (EQ), which ranks higher than IQ-in first place-as a determinant of outstanding job performance.

How can you benefit from knowing this? It's important to assess yourself based on the five dimensions that make up your EQ profile:

Self-perception-Self-regard, self-respect, confidence, actualization and emotional self-awareness

Expression-Communications skills such as assertiveness, showing your feelings and constructive criticism as well as how independent you are

Interpersonal-Participating in mutually satisfying relationships, showing empathy, understanding how others' feel, demonstrating social responsibility and seeing the broader picture.

Decision-making-Problem-solving, controlling your impulses, delaying gratification and being objective Stress management-Flexibility, tolerance, optimism, adaptability, and ability to cope... a key predictor of successful people

What areas are strengths for you, and which are weaknesses? By knowing yourself, and focusing on the things you do well, you can better understand the effect your behavior has on those around you and why you're succeeding (or not) in your chosen career or endeavor. You also have the opportunity to address your weaker areas; it's possible to change your EQ since emotional intelligence seems to be largely learned.

Here's a 10-step plan for developing your EQ

1. Select the skill you want to improve.
2. Test your selection to ensure sustainable motivation.
3. Carefully define the behaviors to change, describing your current behavior and writing a

measurable goal to create a vision of how you'll behave once you've improved in this area.

4. Create a plan to get to your goal.
5. Identify factors that will support and/or hinder your change.
6. Develop self-monitoring systems to assess your progress.
7. Identify potential sources of additional training, experience, and information.
8. Develop feedback systems.
9. Develop self-reward systems.
10. Develop timelines.

Think about individuals you know in "people-oriented" professionals such as financial planning. Do those who are most successful have the most talent-or are they best at being able to relate to other people? You, too, can be a star performer by enhancing your EQ and making the power of emotional intelligence work for you.

EMOTIONAL INTELLIGENCE FOR TODAY'S LEADERS: SELF-AWARENESS

Lately, there has been a lot of press about the importance of emotional intelligence for successful entrepreneurs and leaders.

Recent reports indicate that applicants to Yale's School of Management will be tested on their emotional intelligence.

An entrepreneur and investor with a Harvard MBA published an article in Forbes magazine about the importance of getting an "emotional education" in addition to traditional education.

So what is emotional intelligence and why should leaders cultivate this skill?

Emotional Intelligence (know as "EQ", as opposed to "IQ") is the ability to recognize and control your emotions and then pick up on the emotions of those with whom you are interacting to influence and work effectively with them. It's the ability to express the appropriate emotions at the appropriate time. Emotional Intelligence has been called " a revolutionary, paradigm-shattering idea" (Harvard Business Review) since it is strongly correlated with success.

Having high EQ is the way to get buy-in from the people with whom you are dealing and get them to listen, be engaged and inspired to follow your lead. Research has shown that having high EQ is a better indicator of success than having a high IQ. That is why it is such an important leadership skill The great thing about EQ is that it is a skill set that you can develop to make you a more effective leader. Let's take a closer look.

EQ involves four underlying sets of skills, two having to do with your own emotions and two having to do with the emotions of those around you:

YOU or Personal Competence:

1. **SELF-AWARENESS:** You are aware of your own emotions; and
2. **SELF-MANAGEMENT:** you effectively manage your emotions.
3. **OTHERS or Social Competence:**
4. **SOCIAL AWARENESS:** You can sense the emotions of and empathize with those around you; and
5. **RELATIONSHIP MANAGEMENT:** you know how to interact with, influence and work effectively with other people.

EQ in Practice

Here is how EQ works.

Suppose that you are working closely with a collaborator who makes a lot of demands about how a performance or a presentation is supposed to run. You have just received an email from this person in which she has yet another re□uirement when you thought that everything had been agreed upon.

What would your first impulse be upon receiving this email?

Rather than stewing over this email and sending an explosive response, people with high EQ slow down before reacting. So let's learn some concrete strategies that will enable you to develop high EQ so that you can be on top of your game and know how to use and express your emotions to elicit the best possible results.

It starts with the first of two elements of EQ involving you: Self-Awareness.

EQ Skill #1: Emotional Self-Awareness

Self-awareness is your ability to perceive your own emotions accurately at the moment and understand your tendencies across situations. Self-awareness also means that you can assess the impact of your emotions on those around you. Self-awareness is the first step in developing high EQ because it helps to make sense of your emotions at the moment so that you can formulate the appropriate response.

<u>4 Strategies to Improve Your Self-Awareness</u>

Here are some strategies that you can use to improve your self-awareness.

1. Notice Your Feelings

To become aware of your feelings, it helps to be able to label those emotions. One simple model involves 5 core emotions, with a range of intensity from high to medium to low:

Happiness (elation to cheerfulness to feeling mellow and content)

   Sadness (depressed, somber, disappointed)

   Anger (furious, agitated, irritated)

   Fear (terrified, upset, worried)

   Shame (remorseful, guilty, bashful)

How do you feel about the email from your collaborator?

A good way to develop self-awareness is to notice yourself when you are under stress since this is when you are likely to experience strong emotions. Start labeling those feelings. Notice any uncomfortable body symptoms. Pay attention to your behavior under stress. And keep track of the negative thoughts that accompany these strong emotions.

To develop self-awareness, keep track of your emotions and thoughts, as well as the situations or people that trigger strong emotions. You can do this by sending yourself a text message or an email, writing a post-it note or writing things down in a journal.

2. Accept your feelings

If this email has evoked strong emotions on your part, how do you feel about that?

A lot of people judge their feelings as good or bad. People with high EQ accept their emotions because your emotions give you important clues as to what is going on. For example, if you are angry, something has triggered you. If you are sad, something important may be missing. And of course, if you are happy, pay attention to what is working.

Moreover, by refraining from labeling your emotions and by allowing your emotions to surface, they will run their course and you can move on.

3. Be aware of the impact of your emotions on others

What do you feel like doing in the situation when you receive an email that might cause you to lose it?

Self-awareness also involves observing how your emotions affect others. For example, if you blow up at your fellow collaborator, that behavior will affect the other person as well as everyone else who is present and those people will also be affected, perhaps with a pit their stomachs waiting for you to lash out at them. Over the long run, this will make it harder for people to trust you.

So spend some time reflecting on how your behavior is affecting others. Journaling about such experiences can help you to spot an unhelpful behavior and learn how to control it.

4. Check-in with trusted mentor or friends

A great way to gain self-awareness is to solicit feedback from trusted friends, family members, colleagues or mentors about your behavior. This is especially helpful since we may have a hard time assessing the impact of our behavior on others. Ask for specific examples and situations and be sure to look for patterns. Yes, this takes a lot of courage and by doing so, you are showing yourself and those around you that you are committed to being a trusted colleague and a valuable contributor and leader.

NINE ATTITUDES OF EMOTIONALLY INTELLIGENT LEADERS AND MANAGERS

Emotionally Intelligent Leaders and Managers get the best results!

Like learning to drive, leading and managing people is an experiential journey.

Junior leaders and managers are appointed because they have shown potential, displayed leadership skills or are extremely good in the specific field they are in. More senior leaders and managers can have had a most distinguished career as a professional, i.e. doctor or lawyer or accountant, and the next step for their career is to manage people with the same specialism. An entrepreneurial business owner may be extremely successful and have acquired commercial business acumen and savvy long before they have to employ people.

So people enter leadership and management at all stages. Often their success as a leader or not; will be determined by their people skills, and if these skills haven't had a chance to develop then the most successful entrepreneur or professional may well find the going very tough indeed.

One of the most impactful people skills is emotional intelligence. Wikipedia describes emotional intelligence as" the ability to identify, assess, and control the emotions of oneself, of others, and groups".

If you've ever been in an office where you have seen people have tantrums of a two-year-old or the rumor mill is the most reliable communication channels, or there is a prevalent blame culture, then you know that emotional intelligence is somehow lacking.

Even worse, if the conflict is commonplace, and your people aren't firing on all cylinders or even are openly disengaged then you have may have a problem that stems from limited or unrecognized poor emotional intelligence.

Depending on our psychological profile, and we are all thankfully different; then you may have brilliant emotional intelligence, or conversely you may need to develop this skill more. The great thing about emotional intelligence is that if you are struggling, you can learn!

The first challenge as a young manager was learning how to control your own emotions. In the early years, you'll be often daunted about having to deal with some larger than life characters you'll have to manage. Managing your fear will be one of your first and probably your longest lessons. You might still feel afraid sometimes, but you'll know how to deal with it, and it won't faze me.

The second challenge was to learn how to manage the emotions of your team. This stage was a long one and a steep learning curve. The journey was interesting, thought-provoking and a necessary one.

The final stage in learning might come when you had to think about engaging large teams. Some of who you might not see for months at a time. You try to do the best you could to have physical contact as much as you could humanly manage. Trying to encourage people to feel good, fulfill their potential and understand how much you appreciated them was more difficult. Although there are many skills attached to managing remotely, your own emotional intelligence was a key player in making remote management a success.

The Nine Attitudes are:

1. Accepting people completely for who they are
2. Always looking for the good in people, there is always some
3. Dealing with negatives in an impersonal but practical way and getting over it!
4. Not judging - we all make mistakes.
5. Giving people the benefit of the doubt
6. Listening to what people need and wherever possible - obliging
7. Responding neutrally to anger or other attacking behavior and helping the person to reframe it positively.
8. Pivoting negative situations to achieve a positive outcome.
9. Caring about people, even when they were difficult.

You might be thinking that it all sounds unrealistic, given some of the people you might be managing. But I can guarantee that if you think about it enough, they are all attitudes or stances you would like people to take with you.

Unfortunately, we aren't born with an instruction manual and so navigating and improving our own emotional intelligence often comes through our own life experiences and self-reflection. However, the good news is that there are some clear and easy steps to improving our own emotional intelligence and therefore that of your team and organization.

THE SECRETS OF AN EMOTIONALLY INTELLIGENT ENTREPRENEUR/LEADER

Putting emotional intelligence to work is an emerging trend, not only incorporate leadership but also in entrepreneurship. As an entrepreneur, you cannot rely solely upon your intellectual knowledge. Aside from your IQ, there are a lot of other skills and competencies needed to take your company from a startup to a thriving enterprise. "Entrepreneurs are those that shine and excel in the workplace beyond the norm," according to the study made by Cross and Travaglione of The University of Newcastle, Australia. But really, what sets entrepreneurs apart from the other members of the workforce? Are these characteristics innate, or are they something that can be learned?

Entrepreneurs and leaders are not afraid to express their emotions. They are the kind of people who are expressive and do not withhold information, even their own emotions. This is not only a trait of emotionally intelligent entrepreneurs/leaders, but it's also more of a strategy to resolve issues and conflicts.

Entrepreneurs and leaders know how to regulate their emotions. Being an entrepreneur or leader means you're exposing yourself to a lot of risks and stress. But have you ever wondered why successful entrepreneurs just don't stop despite these negative conditions? It's because they know how to control their emotions. As a result, they "create inspiration and commitment, motivate skills, maintain harmony, and manipulate trust.

Entrepreneurs and leaders use their emotions to solve problems. Starting an enterprise and keeping it alive not only involves risks and stress but also a whole lot of criticism and rejection. According to studies, entrepreneurs tend to transform negative feelings such as criticism and rejection into a motive for improvement. These highly self-motivated individuals use their feelings as a source of determination and relentlessness to avoid a repeat of such rejection and criticism.

Emotionally intelligent entrepreneurs and leaders have a high level of self-awareness. These individuals are well-grounded yet confident. They know what they want and what they can do. Their knowledge of their self-efficacy helps them decide on matters that could affect the business, no matter how big or small the impact is. Being an excellent decision-maker sets these breed of individuals apart from the regular members of the workforce.

Entrepreneurs are socially adept. In entrepreneurship, an entrepreneur is often faced with situations that require persuasion and negotiation skills. They tend to use their social skills to their advantage, like getting people to agree with them or do business with them. This talent starts from their smart ways of building a network of people they know, trust, and like before they even need anything from them. No wonder they often get what they want!

EI SMART entrepreneurs know how to effectively empathize. In the past, researchers define entrepreneurs as opportunists and creators of opportunities that they can exploit (Littunen, 2000). But really, entrepreneurs are more than that. They are not only good at creating opportunities, but they are also good at showing empathy to others, especially the people they work with. They know how to build, cultivate, and promote rapport among employees and clients.

Now, who says that emotions are unimportant in the business? Of course, they are! Your emotions, whether positive or negative, can influence your judgment, memory recall, ability to show appreciation, creativity, and reasoning skills. It's important as well to take note that entrepreneurs were not born with these traits. These characteristics were developed over time, thanks to experience. Also, it's good to know that these strategies can be learned. Nobody expects you to have all six characteristics mentioned above. Now, ask yourself, "Am I ready to learn about EI and be an emotionally intelligent entrepreneur?"

WHAT BEING EMOTIONALLY INTELLIGENT DOES NOT MEAN

An Emotionally Intelligent person has been described as one who has discovered the most effective way to CONTROL and USE his/her emotions to achieve improvements in performance and learning. From the above, one can correctly infer that the ability to CONTROL and USE one's emotions to actualize set goals is what will make a person qualify to be called Emotionally Intelligent.

The key attributes/qualities an Emotionally Intelligent person would typically display such as:

1. Ability to motivate him/herself towards achieving a set purpose(s).
2. Ability to persevere in spite of adversity of frustration i.e. things going wrong.
3. Ability to control impulses and delay gratification i.e. postpone immediate enjoyment to secure a long term goal e.g. financial security.
4. Mental Stamina evidenced by the ability to regulate one's moods and keep distressed from swamping one's ability to think.
5. Ability to have empathy i.e. be sensitive to the feelings or emotions of others.
6. Ability to get along with other people.
7. Ability to get into "flow" or "the zone".

Emotional Intelligence Can Be Taught

It is generally agreed that unlike IQ which cannot be changed much by education, most crucial emotional competencies can be learned and improved upon - if they are taught - especially from childhood.

Academic intelligence offers almost no preparation for the shades of adversity or opportunities that life's experiences will bring.

There is however a problem with how some people have quickly latched on to/used the argument that academic ability/IQ is not a guarantee of success in life. They loudly pronounce "getting along with others" as a critical skill/emotional competence essential for social success.

While I acknowledge that "interpersonal skill" is indeed an essential skill, my observations of some of those who emphasize this "getting along with others" to succeed, makes me worry that they think it must be done at all and ANY cost.

In other words, INTEGRITY and SINCERITY of purpose/intent are NOT given any consideration.

Now the major danger inherent in this kind of thinking is that it inadvertently confers a cloak of credibility on insincere and manipulative individuals who exploit their social relationships for selfish ends. (E.g. to look good or gain wide approval from everyone they consider important or relevant).

That is why I believe it is important to identify specific instances when "getting along with others" does not translate to being Emotionally Intelligent in the TRUE sense of the expression.

The Anchorless Social Chameleon

To describe certain individuals in society who are champions at making good impressions. They are typically driven by a need to earn the approval of others at almost any cost - in my opinion, a negative manifestation of "getting along with others". I say negative because it is devoid of INTEGRITY.

Below I now provide a specific example of the behavior such individuals would exhibit:

Saying One Thing & Doing Another. Having no independent opinion. Lacking the ability (or willingness) to assert themselves EVEN when the need is obvious or apparent.

They are obsessed with "madly trying to fit in with whosoever they are with"(Re: Goleman). They do this by actively checking those they relate with for signs of what they like or want, before making a response. For instance, they would voice an opinion "guided" by what they know (or think) the person they are with wants to hear. To get along and be liked, they are willing to make people they dislike think they are friendly with them. (I consider this an UNFULFILLING way to live life - at the mercy of every whim and caprice of others!).

the ability to "get along" in the manner described above can be quite useful in some professions (e.g. diplomacy, sales, trial law, etc). However, in "normal" society, where having integrity, sincerity, and a CONSCIENCE are (hopefully) valued, the need to strike a healthy balance between having "social polish" for getting along with others and being TRUE to oneself becomes imperative.

Anyone who loses sight of the fact that having EMOTIONAL INTEGRITY is more important and essential THAN winning social approval, does him/herself a great disservice in the long term.

To be true to yourself, and NOT be a Social Chameleon, or to have emotional integrity, you would - regardless of the possible social consequences - be willing to employ non-combative confrontation as the need may arise (and it always DOES now and then in life) to tackle any appearances of "duplicity or denial" you detect in those you relate with. The foregoing is NOT something the Social Chameleon would ever attempt - for obvious reasons.

FINAL WORDS

It is my considered opinion that the ability to maintain relationships and keep friends depends on whatever may be the prevailing socio-cultural values in society as they compare with the individual's morals/values, principles, conscience, etc.

Consider a society in which dissemination based on race, gender, tribe, ethnicity, etc exist as defined by, say, a ruling class.

You (and your offspring's) ability to succeed (financially, educationally, etc) to a large extent in that environment will depend on how the prevalent discrimination rules affect you. If they favor you (E.g. you belong to the favored group), then you are more are likely to succeed. If they don't, then you could be "doomed" to failure!

In the latter instance, the □uestion would be how far out on a limb would you be willing to go to challenge such discrimination and fight for redress against those who established it and who hold/use power. This □uestion must be considered against the likely negative consequences which could results - such as a possible loss or your freedom and even friends!

Nelson Mandela through his struggle against apartheid provides us an excellent reference case in point, that illustrates the conse□uences mentioned in the preceding paragraph.

Put the □uestion this way: How well would you be able to get along with others if you embarked on just but widely unpopular campaigns such as the above? To dogmatically apply the "getting along with others" to succeed, you would have to compromise your values, principles, and beliefs (e.g. close your eyes to racial injustices) to "keep" your friendships with those who do things you disapprove of.

Essentially, I am saying a certain "conducive" societal situation is re□uired for effective application of the Emotional Intelligence of "getting along with others" to occur.

THE ONE THING YOU NEED TO SUCCEED AS AN ENTREPRENEUR/LEADER

I am lucky enough to know some very successful entrepreneurs and leaders and it is clear they share certain characteristics. Interestingly from a creative point of view, the majority of the most successful tend to be dyslexic which means they develop other skills to compensate, particularly those of verbal recall and a high level of emotional intelligence in reading people and situations.

Now some new research from the University of Maryland has pointed up the fact that general intelligence is not enough - though entrepreneurs have that in spades usually. Another essential skill is to have practical intelligence as that can mean the difference between entrepreneurial success or failure.

Psychologists have identified multiple kinds of intelligence, but this study indicates that how much practical intelligence a person has is a good indicator of likely entrepreneurial success.

So what is practical intelligence?

According to J. Robert Baum, Director of Entrepreneurship Research at the University of Maryland, practical intelligence is "an experience-based accumulation of skills and explicit knowledge as well as the ability to apply that knowledge to solve everyday problems." That is a very academic way of saying what you or I might refer to as plain old-fashioned know-how or common sense.

It is all about learning from your experiences in life and that is something that entrepreneurs excel at. To begin a successful business venture you must have the practical intelligence necessary to relate your previous experience to what is now needing to be done. Practical intelligence is the result of an experimental hands-on operating style that leads to specific learning and that usually means those with high practical intelligence tend to develop useful knowledge by doing and learning, not by watching or reading. In other words, they are active, not passive in their learning style.

But can practical intelligence explain why some are successful and others are not? Yes, to some degree, it can and an example is by looking at people with strong general intelligence who still fail at business and those who didn't do so well academically but who still succeed beyond their - and their teachers -wildest dreams.

There are many kinds of intelligence, including emotional, social and creative. Practical intelligence is just one, but a critical one for entrepreneurial success. Other factors are personal characteristics that are important in venture creation and growth such as the way entrepreneurs typically have confidence in what they are undertaking and have the ability to make quick decisions and take action. They are also willing to use their knowledge or what they have learned to experiment and try new approaches to improve the process or product.

Practical intelligence is gained by learning from past experiences and using that knowledge to enhance their enterprise, or in other words not being afraid to make mistakes and learn from them. Taking a creative approach to life and its challenges are some of the best ways to build on your innate practical intelligence so look at everything you do as an opportunity, not a problem.

DEVELOPING YOUR EMOTIONAL INTELLIGENCE IS VITAL FOR LOVE, PEACE, AND JOY IN LIFE

What is emotional intelligence?

There is wisdom that becomes available to us when we recognize that there is intelligence inside us that empowers us to be able to manage our own emotions and to know that our emotions are our own. This is to say that we are a hundred percent responsible for how we feel and not anyone else. When we understand that our emotions are simply our own reactions to a given situation and not the doing of some external forces, we essentially stop playing the victim and begin to take responsibility for how we feel. The ability to identify and manage our own emotions and to understand the emotions of people around us is emotional intelligence.

This intelligence follows four stages: Self-awareness, self-management, social awareness, and relationship management. The first two stages have to do with understanding our behavior and ourselves. The last two stages underline the importance of understanding others, and their behavior.

Success does not create happiness and love in life.

The notion that success creates happiness is often followed by statements like 'When I achieve this, only then will I finally be happy', for there are many successful people, given that our idea of success is often determined in monitory terms, who lack love and are not happy at all. So if success does not create happiness and love, then what does? The answer lies within the core emotional intelligence.

At the core of emotional intelligence is self-awareness.

Adam smith once said, "The first thing you have to know is yourself. A man who knows himself can step outside himself and watch his own reactions like an observer." At the core of knowing 'thyself' is taking responsibility for all that you are and so if success does not create love and happiness in your life, then being responsible for your own love and happiness along emotional intelligence does.

What does it mean to be self-aware?

To be self-aware simply is to be conscious of your thoughts, attitudes, behavior, and emotions, to have a clear understanding of all that makes you who you are and to be able to manage and control those feelings.

There is a rather simple way of managing these emotions. In a world system where every individual has overstimulated with thousands of bits of information flooding the mind, a path to gaining control over the mind is simply to come to a space of feeling safe and relaxed. The concept of meditation, known to man by many adjectives like contemplation, introspection, rumination or reflection, is simply bringing the mind to a relaxed altered state of awareness where things appear to make sense, where the mind is no longer flooded but is calm and observant of the very thoughts and emotions that are otherwise is overwhelming.

To any form of meditation there are three common signals to the brain; first is to close the eyes, the second to focus on slow deep breaths and the third is to relax all muscle tension in the body. With doing this follows a profound realization that one is responsible and has conscious control over his thoughts and feelings.

If we are responsible for how we feel, then why do we feel hurt?

Blaming others for hurting us is simply like blaming someone for poking you in a place that was already bruised. It is not the poking alone that hurts, but it is simply poking at the bruise that hurts. Similarly, all of us are emotionally bruised as a result of our past circumstances, and when people poke at those places, we can either continue blaming the person saying they hurt us, or continue to get hurt on the same bruise time and again, or just heal the bruise instead. Healing the bruise instead is taking responsibility for how you feel, dropping the idea that other people are responsible for your love and happiness.

In conclusion, to be emotionally intelligent is to be self-aware, empowering ourselves and owning the responsibility for our own feelings of love and happiness instead of playing constant victim to the world outside us. Therefore, being emotionally intelligent will reveal to you real peace and happiness, as long as you choose to create it because how you feel is how you decide to feel.

DEVELOPING EMOTIONAL INTELLIGENCE TO HELP YOU AND YOUR ORGANIZATION

Most entrepreneurs and leaders are skilled at starting things - they keep pushing to move a project forward, but they sometimes realize that it's not working, so they go back to the beginning and start over. As a leader, you know that it is important to make sure the concepts of vision, alignment, and execution are entrenched in your mind. Doing so makes it possible to build and grow instead of being caught in the familiar feedback loop that always ends up at square one. This is where the concept of emotional intelligence, or EQ, becomes important. When you think of the most successful leaders of organizations ranging from startups to Fortune 500 companies, almost all of them have worked very hard on developing their EQs. There are very few great leaders in the world who haven't developed a refined EQ. At the very least, they realize that EQ is something important to work on.

The majority of leaders possess some kind of technical skill in a specific area, but they work incredibly hard on the emotional intelligence aspect of life. Following are six key points that leaders are encouraged to consider to develop emotional intelligence more fully:

Be receptive to input regarding how you can improve. As a leader, you understand the bottom line - it all begins and ends with you. Meet with your board, visit with your peers and speak with your managers to receive an honest assessment. It is crucial to be able to understand the areas in which you can improve.

Take a look at ways you can help your managers. Think about methods for coaching them and fostering improvement. Also, think about how you can improve your assessments. After all, if you aren't willing to realize something is broken, how is it possible for you to fix it? Think about different areas where there's room for improvement, and don't be afraid to use an outside set of eyes.

View leadership as a program of continuous improvement. There is never an arrival or a destination. The great basketball coach John Wooden has said, "It's what you learn after you know everything that counts." You simply never arrive.

Understand that no individual can ever be great at everything. Of course, you might be more adept at the vision side of things, or perhaps you are more skilled when it comes to alignment or execution. You might be better at one thing, but you have to realize that it is necessary to improve in other aspects as you develop your team intending to fill in gaps. One important key is to be open and honest about developmental needs and your weaknesses. Admitting your shortcomings is not a liability; it is, in fact, a strength because everyone understands that you possess those weaknesses anyway. Admit them at the outset, and do what it is necessary to prepare your team to fill the gaps.

Communicate your message over and over again.

Traditional, conventional performance management no longer exists. If you want to consider your vision while creating alignment and enabling execution, you need to think of alternative methods for communicating those concepts to the people in your organization. Eliminate annual reviews, which often don't occur at 12-month intervals anyway. Instead, create a mechanism through which real-time feedback can be given and received. This creates alignment, plus it inspires your team. Additionally, it allows you to give and receive feedback so you can ensure that your vision is understood, and it gives you the structure that you require for success. These concepts are essential to developing healthy emotional intelligence, which can have a positive impact on every aspect of your organization.

MISSION ACCOMPLISHED: THE POWER OF NEUROPLASTICITY & EMOTIONAL INTELLIGENCE TO ACHIEVE GOALS

Realizing your dreams takes vision, action, commitment, and a plan with a path to the finish line.

Whether you're setting goals to start a new business, or simply to motivate your professional team, success depends on developing a strategic plan that supercharges your goals and gets them from mere objectives to Mission Accomplished.

From small entrepreneurs, women in business, to top-level CEOs, goal setting is a tool used by most top achievers in every field, however many of us find goal setting challenges.

Now that's about to change, thanks to new cutting edge techniques in Neuroplasticity, a revolutionary brain-science that teaches us how to harness the power of the brain to activate our Emotional Intelligence to achieve our goals.

Most of us are aware of SMART goals, an acronym for the five steps of Specific, Measurable, Achievable, Relevant, and Time-based goals. It's a simple tool used by businesses to go beyond the realm of fuzzy goal-setting into actionable plans for results-but it's also very "left-brain" in its approach. To fast-track our goals we need the "right-brain" put into action as well, allowing us to tap into and engage our Emotional Intelligence--our imagination, creativity, and emotions-- creating a balanced and integrated approach.

That's were Neuroplasticity comes into play.

Neuroplasticity refers to the brain's ability to change, creating new neural pathways and synapses in light of experience--and this change is generated not only by real-life experience but by visualization and imagination as well.

Research confirms the power of imagination to light up our brains in the same way as if we were doing. Using self-directed Neuroplasticity techniques, new neural pathways are created when we focus our attention towards the desired outcome--whether that's learning to play an instrument or succeeding in business--contributing significantly to optimizing the "mind-set" for achieving our goals.

The key is developing our Emotional Intelligence.

Creativity and visualization are core components of it, but it also means being cognizant of and managing our emotions, as for better or worse, emotions, especially sustained ones, drive us in powerful ways. They also have the power to intuitively guide us and to change every aspect of our being--from the tiniest cells in our bodies to the largest neural synaptic pathways of our brains.

We develop Emotional Intelligence not only through creativity, imagination, and visualization but also by adopting principles of mindfulness--training our minds to stay focused, present, detached and objective as well as by listening to that inner voice that speaks to us from our deepest intuitive core.

Practicing these techniques we see Neuroplasticity in action, and our brains can change in as little as just a few weeks--substantially enough to even be seen on a brain scan.

When we set your goals using a whole-brain approach, we harness the full power of Neuroplasticity to activate Emotional Intelligence to achieve our goals. Give it daily attention and see how quickly goals come to life.

THE NATURE OF INTELLIGENCE

First of all, intelligence is not fixed at birth. It can and should be developed throughout life from childhood to old age.

Second. Intelligence does not deteriorate with age. We do not lose 30,000 brain cells every day, or every time we have a beer or a whiskey, though an excess of alcohol or drugs can cause brain cell deterioration so too can the stress hormone cortisol.

Third. Intelligence isn't even a single entity. I identified 7 different types of intelligence, two in the left hemisphere of the brain, what I call the masculine brain and five on the right hemisphere, what I call the feminine brain. The masculine intelligence is maths/logic and linguistics and until the mid-'80s were still regarded as the only intelligence worth having. The school system is based on them. Gardner eventually recognized an 8th intelligence, spirituality now called naturalistic IQ, based in the right hemisphere. Below is the full list. See if you recognise yourself.

Our 8 IQs

Linguistic - well developed in people who are good with words, who like to write and read a lot. Examples: authors, journalists, orators, and comedians.

Mathematical/Logical - well developed in people who are good with numbers and appreciate step-by-step, logical explanations. Examples: engineers, economists, scientists, lawyers, and accountants.

Visual/Spatial - well developed in people who are good at art, visualizing, navigating. Examples: architects, photographers, painters, strategic planners, and sculptors.

Musical - well developed in people who are good at music and rhyme, and who have a natural rhythm. Examples: composers, musicians, and recording engineers.

Bodily/Physical - well developed in people who are good at sport, dance, and handicrafts. Examples: athletes, sportspersons, carpenters, surgeons, builders.

Interpersonal - well developed in people who are good at persuading, selling, teaching others, and who can read other people's moods well. Examples: teachers, trainers, politicians, religious leaders, salespeople.

Intra-Personal or Reflective - well developed in people who are good at self-analysis and reflection, concluding their own experience (and mistakes!), setting goals and making plans. Examples are philosophers, psychologists, therapists, entrepreneurs. People who make things happen.

Naturalistic - well developed in people who like and respect nature and are interested in subjects like astronomy, evolution and the environment. Examples: farmers, vets, biologists, gardeners, and environmentalists.

Do you recognize your strongest intelligence from the list?

Finally, and perhaps the most startling point of all. Women are potentially far more intelligent than men. That statement isn't 100% true. It should read: Feminine thinkers are potentially more intelligent than masculine thinkers, because feminine and masculine in this case cut across the genders of male and female.

The most obvious example of this was Margaret Thatcher, a very masculine, machine-like thinker. Her strictly utilitarian, in feminine approach to problems, though successfully economically, did considerable social damage to the UK from which we are still suffering today. The late Carl Sagan, on the other hand, was primarily a feminine thinker, despite being a scientist. He was brilliant, charming and worked tirelessly for the benefit of humanity.

Feminine of course, in the context of thinking, should not be confused with effeminate or female. Many men are born right hemisphere dominant. The theatre, the music industry, advertising, and films are full of right-brain dominant men.

Of our eight bits of intelligence six are on the feminine right side of the brain, our creative intelligence. They can handle information at the rate of one and one quarter million bits of information per second i.e. 1,250,000 bits per second whereas the poor old masculine brain can only handle forty bits per second, yes 40, four zero.

Masculine thinking is straight-lined, sequential, non-emotional and thinks in words. Feminine thinking is flexible, has depth and breadth, is creative, emotional and almost limitless in its imaginative properties and it thinks in pictures, which is why it's so much faster. A picture tells a thousand words. Masculine thinking demands one task at a time whereas feminine thinking allows multi-tasking. The BBC program Panorama did a program in 1997 called the Future is Female. What they meant is The Future is Feminine. They failed to take into account a large number of feminine male thinkers.

School Failures

From all this new research has sprung three new terms: Whole-brain Learning i.e. Accelerated Learning; and its consequence, Integrated Intelligence. Whole-brain Learning is the Left and Right Hemisphere (brain) working together but because the Right Brain is so much faster it is dominant. Despite this, the majority of school failures are Right Brain Dominant. They are misunderstood and often put down by a largely Left Brain teaching staff as being lazy and difficult. They often end up withdrawn or downright disruptive.

Right Brain pupils, especially boys, are sensitive, creative daydreamers who take failure and criticism very badly, unlike their left-brain counterparts who are much less emotionally affected by other people's perception of them.

What is Intelligence?

Intelligence is the linking of brain cells (neurons) by connective tissue known as dendrites. The gaps between the connecting dendrites are known as synapses (the synaptic gap). Everyone is born with 12 to 15 thousand million, brain cells, each cell capable of holding information. But each cell can make up to 100,000 connections to other cells and it's those connections, which effectively make up Intelligence. The more cells which are connected the more information we can work with and the more ideas we can come up with. Effectively the more synapses we have the greater our intelligence. Unfortunately, much of our Right Brain creativity is being killed off by an overabundance of Left Brain training at school or by many university courses.

Live Longer

What this means is that everyone on the planet has the same intellectual potential. It means also that there is no such thing as stupidity, only levels of intelligence, all of which can be developed up to the day we die. Indeed, if stupidity exists at all, it exists as a defense mechanism. It also means that age is no barrier to intellectual development. On the contrary, the more we keep our brain active, the longer we are likely to live, i.e. healthy mind, healthy body.

Expectations

Expectations are crucial in any field of development, but especially in education. If you expect something to happen, you are already halfway to achieving it. The American psychologist Rosenthal divided a class in two, following a series of class IQ tests. He told the teacher he had divided the class into two halves according to the results, bright on the left, less bright on the right, but not to tell them why they were thus divided and above all, not to treat them differently.

Eight months later the class results of the 'brighter' group were up by 30%, even their IQ tests scored higher. Incredible really as Rosenthal had chosen the names for the original lists at random, but because the teacher expected the 'brighter' group to do better, as much as she tried, she unwittingly conveyed this message to them over the months following Rosenthal dividing the class. She also conveyed the opposite view to the other half of the class.

For this reason, all teachers must be made aware of the new research which offers neurological evidence, that all intelligence can be developed. Without question, some of us are natural mathematicians, or musicians or organizers or writers, but all of us can and should develop the weaker parts of our intellect to bring them up to at least average.

Social Conditioning and Lack of Confidence

One major reason for poor academic achievement is the switch from really trying to make the grade, to looking as if you have already made the grade. We're talking image building here. Even those who are making the grade as footballers, pop stars, etc get caught up in teenage image building where the loudmouth and super cool swagger replace reality. False confidence often bordering on arrogance masks the reality of fear, lack of confidence and low self-esteem. This means individuals never solve their problems therefore never move on because their attitude is, problems? What problems? So how can you begin to solve what isn't (perceived) to be there?

This is all perfectly understandable under the circumstances, but unfortunately, by not facing up to the problems of lack of confidence, low self-esteem, and poor educational standards, it hinders the progress of intellectual development.

To overcome any problem we must, first of all, recognize that the problem exists. Parents and teachers must find ways of encouraging their children to learn without putting them under unnecessary pressure or trying to terrify them into working. Parents and teachers must find ways of learning how to relax so they don't over-react to their children's normal mistakes by shouting and they should never physically hit their children for making mistakes. That is so counterproductive.

Parents must continue to stretch their own intellectual potential at every opportunity to lead their children by example. Love, kindness, and gentleness should be by words in all schools and homes. All children need that. All children deserve that. You deserve that. You also deserve the joy this new approach will bring to your homes and communities.

Defense Mechanisms

Every Human Being is programmed to learn. Therefore any child who shirks the learning process is doing so because his inner defense mechanisms, over which he has no control, have been set up to protect him from further emotional hurt. They are designed to shield him from the pain of failure, which he is experiencing during the learning process. Let us all adopt these simple concepts:

Failure is OK. It's part of the Learning Process.

And

Mistakes are our Best Friends.

The only people who don't fail are those who never try. We learn from our mistakes, pick ourselves up and try again. And when our students make a mistake let's not be too ready to point it out before first pointing up the part of the answer they have got right e.g. 95% correct, but just a little mistake here, rather than: WRONG! With the emphasis on the mistake and completely ignoring the bits, he got right. Let's remember that children are easily hurt. Indeed. Are even we as adults not easily hurt if we look silly in front of others? But who's perfect? People, especially the young should always be given credit for trying and if they fail they should be encouraged to have another go and helped where possible to succeed next time.

Teachers Fail as well as Students

Because everyone can learn and is programmed to do so, anyone who is failing to learn is not being taught properly. If our students aren't picking ideas up, isn't it up to us as educators and/or parents to find another way of presenting the information? Humans aren't machines all programmed exactly the same way. We now know there are numerous learning styles, which we should all become familiar with.

Student failure is a failure of communication between educators and students. It's the educator's job to find a way of communicating his information to the student. Accelerated Learning Techniques, which are now available to schools via Classroom Resources in Bristol, can overcome any problems with spelling, tables or reading. We have no excuse for not having the tools to overcome our problems as communicators.

Anxiety Problems

As a therapist in the 70's and '80s working in the field of dyslexia and slow learners I soon discovered that all of the students, irrespective of age or background, were being hampered by anxiety or the second stage anxiety, tension. I used visualization to help the under 12's (The Magic Garden) and hypnosis for the over 12's (The Study Relaxer). The techniques were not only successful in calming the students down (including stopping bed wetting, nightmares and sleepwalking within days) they also produced dramatic improvements in the learning process.

Modern research shows why. The seat of short-term memory is in the Limbic System, i.e. midbrain. It also controls, among other things, the emotions. When the emotions are upset, the brain switches to fight or flight mode during which time little or no learning can take place until the student is calm again. Fear is the enemy of learning, whether the student is 5 or 55. More frightening is the permanent damage which the stress hormone cortisol can do to the Hippocampus, an integral part of laying down new memories.

Up to 40% of the Hippocampus can be destroyed by prolonged stress

Almost everyone who has learning difficulties is right-brain dominant, i.e. big-picture thinkers. They prefer to see the big picture first then fill in the details as they go along. Despite the right side of the brain being far more powerful than the left, RB children fall behind at school because they can't pick up on the details of tables and spellings. They appear 'stupid' whilst often being far more intelligent than their 'cleverer' LB classmates.

The first thing these damages is confidence and self-esteem, without which learning is much more difficult. After a short while on this downward spiral, they begin to lose hope and give up. The Edinburgh Techniques, developed in the mid-'80s for children of the rich and famous (as it turned out), are based on Whole-brain Learning which is Right Brain dominant, allowing even 7-year-old dyslexics to spell words like Psychiatrist and Encyclopedia in the first session. (Because the technique is visually based, students, can also spell the words backward. That has to be seen to be believed. If anything shows they are not stupid, spelling PSYCHIATRIST backwards does.) The best then goes onto learning a technique for the 12 times table (up to 12 x 19) in the same session.

Every one of us has the same intellectual potential, but not the same Intellectual abilities. I can give a speech in front of thousands of people from only a few notes and keep the audience interested and amused for 2 or 3 hours. I can organize and run political campaigns with ease. I have a good grasp of BIG subjects like politics and psychology but I am slow at learning languages and other detailed subject matter. Engineering and maths beyond 10th grade leave me cold. Many of you reading this will say no, maths is easy, it's logical. You can check your work. There are guidelines. I don't know how you can work with such amorphous subjects like politics and psychology.

The reason for the differences in the way our intelligence link up and whether we are right hemisphere dominant or left, people-orientated or fact orientated.

Two important facts to bear in mind are these:

One: It is never too late to take up or resume learning. All learning makes the brain progressively better.

Two: Information in itself is not intelligence. Intelligence is the use of information not the gathering of it.

Finally. As we move through the 21st-century change will become even faster and more complicated. We must always be ready to move with the times. No generation in history is right about everything. Even the most deeply held beliefs of past generations are ridiculous. Spare the rod and spoil the child belongs in the 19th century and has no place in modern society. If we can't lead our children to the Promised Land we certainly aren't going to be able to beat them into it. Let's take off the pressure. Let's encourage and applaud the effort. Let's try and be more understanding of the difficulties of our students. Let's remember to accentuate the positives, not the negatives and we will all be amazed and delighted with the results.

FIVE SECRETS TO GREATER PRODUCTIVITY FOR ENTREPRENEURS AND LEADERS

These techniques have been under trial for several years by some of the most successful online entrepreneurs that have the freedom of working from home but have whittled away at creating the perfect formula for productivity. These are imperative techniques for the greatest productivity and higher profits for your business. Now let's get started.

#1: SCHEDULE THE OVERWHELM

This may seem like a no-brainer but how often do we consistently schedule everything? Whether you are a corporate executive, a small business entrepreneur or a stay-at-home business owner, it's easy to get overwhelmed by the sheer volume of information we receive daily. If we're trying to learn something new as well as manage the tasks we must complete in a given day, it can truly feel....well, overwhelming! This is compounded if we are not scheduling properly.

First, you must realize that feeling overwhelmed is a good thing. That's right - a good thing! It's better than being underwhelmed, which often means underpaid. Whenever we're pushing ourselves towards a worthy accomplishment, we should expect to overwhelm. Here are some tips for scheduling your days and managing the overwhelm in your business:

- Schedule time to manage your information overload. Don't do it on the fly -reactive- or when you feel like it. Put it on your calendar. Yes, have a 4-hour chunk of time where you answer emails, get on Facebook and let in the natural distractions. The other times of the day? Don't deal with emails, Facebook or texts.
- Schedule time to disconnect. Completely disconnect from social media, phones, email, even family. Have an idea day where you spend at least a couple of hours being creative and relaxed once a week. Get focused on what you want to learn and become.
- Don't multitask. Focus on one thing at a time.
- Don't get emotionally attached! Don't take it personally if you feel overwhelmed.
- Got off track? Get right back on track and don't even think about feeling guilty or wasting time thinking about "what if" or "I should have". Get passed it mentally and move on.
- Schedule days devoted to specific actions/tasks. For example, Monday & Thursdays are devoted to calls. Friday: Money-making activity. Wednesday: Afternoon is catch-up time, like all the magazines, newsletters, etc.
- Have a start and finish time for every action. This cannot be stressed enough here! Have an end time or else you'll work on it all day. This is the opposite of being disciplined and will lose your money faster than you can make it. Are you ready for more?

#2: JOURNAL IT!

This is a nice way of saying, "Keep a detailed schedule". Please keep the groaning down and hear me out on this one. The benefits far outweigh the 10 minutes a day it will take to do this and I have a great tip on how to do it right.

Keeping track of your day does two massive things at one time. First, it gets you into a disciplined mindset where you can predict and rely on the fact that most every morning you are going to spend 3 hours doing the only high-leverage, money-generating activity. Writing this down every night and filling it in with finer detail about what you need to accomplish will drive you to do it.

The second bonus to journaling each day's activities is that you can go back at the end of the week and see what did and did not work. Hi-lite the shortcomings where you dropped off the deep end and got caught up in answering phone calls because you were spending your three hours of money generating activity in your office. You can then ask yourself if it's a better idea to find a place without a phone.

Make sure to check back in a month or so and take stock of your activity. There are always holes that can be filled. Maybe you see yourself spending 5 hours every day on one activity and it didn't turn out the profits you'd hoped for. Hi-lite it. Analyze it. Could you have done something differently? This is where the journaling pays off.

Writing your activity out, organizing and reporting it not only enables you to see what the heck is going on with your days, but it also gives you perspective and puts emotional space between you and your work activity. A big point not to miss is...

"Don't get emotionally attached to the overwhelming and distractions."

By writing your activities daily you can step back and look at it logically and with less emotional attachment. Some emotional attachment examples are feeling frustrated, lack of enthusiasm, feelings of being totally lost in all the information coming at you.

Keep writing and you'll see the big monster broken down into tiny bits leaving you feeling like the victor. Let's now move onto something even more important.

#3: MANAGING DISTRACTIONS & INTERRUPTIONS

Allowing things to distract you is O.K. - when you schedule it! Schedule the distractions in and schedule them out.

What are you ALLOWING into your environment to distract you? People, email, phone calls, texts, social media?

I noticed recently that as soon as I open up my laptop, like a well-worn path through the woods, I automatically open up my email. Not my work email has you, but my email where I am notorious for writing long email responses to friends. Here's how I stopped myself:

I now schedule the time for my email. When I am scheduled for high-profit activities like writing ad copy I open the computer and go straight to Word, not Google docs because I'll see the email and I will read it. I then copy/paste my writing from Word into a Google doc, taking just seconds to do and averting the email rabbit hole.

Distractions and overwhelm are here to stay. We have to change our viewpoint.

"You can't always change the view but you can change your viewpoint"

Changing your viewpoint entails looking at overwhelming as a positive. Imagine with me if you were underwhelmed i.e. sitting on the couch doing nothing and you know what that equates to? Underwhelmed = Underpaid.

Think of overwhelm as a friend that simply needs to be scheduled in and managed. Set up boundaries and rules to omit distractions. Take note of distractions. What are they and when do they crop up? Put up boundaries to deflect these.

Take note that the morning, no matter how groggy you seem to be at first, is your most productive time of the day and needs to be dedicated to a high-yielding activity

- Set up boundaries and rules to omit distractions.
- Take note of distractions. What are they and when?
- First in the morning have a power/nutrition drink, the phone should be off from the night before still. This is your MOST productive time, best revenue-producing time. Somewhere between 7:30 and 11:00. 3 hours.
- Second, go work out.
- Third: Sometime after 12:30 or 1 PM deal with all the distractions: calls, email, text, etc., but only on Mondays and Wednesdays.
- Need to learn new skills. Must set time aside for this. Block it out and treat it like going to school. Find the perfect environment.
- How do you become aware of the distractions? We're unconscious. What's annoying? Ask if the distraction is aligned with your goals. Is this making money? How much money are you losing right now because of the distraction?
- Schedule the distractions. Be open to them because they are not going away. What is taking your attention away?

#4: IMPORTANCE OF ENVIRONMENT

Setting the stage for your greater productivity might top this list of five. Where you sit to accomplish your tasks permeates the tasks themselves, how you perform, what you think and most importantly if you are open to those new million-dollar ideas.

Let's get to it here by starting with your scheduled distraction time when you are answering emails and returning phone calls, maybe doing some social media. This is best suited to your home office. Sounds obvious and dull, however, it's more interesting to note that the home office should not be used for anything else you do. Let me explain.

When you are doing creative work like writing, brainstorming or creating a presentation with beautiful diagrams or animation the home office presents you with dangerous time-sucking distractions. The culprits are ringing phones and that feeling that you need to be getting as much stuff done as fast as you can so you can check it off the list.

To do creative work its highly suggested to sit in a room with a nice view, relaxed seating, a laptop that doesn't have your browser window open and a cup of your favorite drink. If you work at home maybe it's the dining room table or outside on the porch.

There is also the all-important study time. You must spend at least one night a week keeping up on new trends, learning a new skill and reading for the sole purpose of elevating your intelligence and performance. The perfect environment for learning?

Everyone is different, however, studies show that a good old fashioned replica of a classroom is best. Keep it sterile, no distractions and even blank walls with no windows. Not for everyone. It's suggested because it keeps you alert, focused and ready to absorb information. Libraries, a quiet corner at Barnes & Noble or a sterile space with little stimuli will do. When is there a shortage of stimuli?

Later at night when things settle down for the day is good for the night owls. If you are an early bird the quietest hour that meditation gurus get up is 4 AM. Try that on for size.

One last idea that I heard from a successful businessman was this: "If you need ideas to communicate with the world then go be in the world."

Schedule it and repeat it over and over again. Repetition of good habits breeds excellence. Now we're at #5 and the most valuable piece of information so keep reading.

#5: PLACE A MONETARY VALUE ON YOUR TIME

Here's a fun trick that will motivate you. Nothing like a good dose of motivation, right? Here it is:

Next time you find yourself wasting away the minutes or even the hours get yourself on track by thinking about the hundreds of dollars slipping away. Using the Dan Kennedy Formula you can calculate exactly how much money is being lost. Calculate it like this:

If your goal is to make $200,000 this year that is 250 workdays a year and 3 hours of productive/profitable time spent a day (yes, you read that right, 3 hours and I'll explain later) and this equals 750 real work hours a year totaling $267 per hour.

How do you view your hours now? You don't want to lose the money, right? It's all about being disciplined and focused on your goals.

Let's go over that confusing three hours of productive time a day. Don't shake your head too hard in the negative because the experts have discovered that 3 hours is exactly how much time professionals and executives are productive in a single day. Productive meaning money producing hours. Chatting on the phone about this morning's meeting is not productive hours.

Take a moment right now to calculate your hourly worth. Then go back to the schedule you have created for yourself and see where you can shut down those unproductive hours.

- Takeaways:
    - Don't complain, manage it.
    - Calculate your hourly value right now and every year.
    - Can't manage time only manage yourself in time.
    - Schedule the distractions.
    - ALWAYS schedule a beginning and an ending to everything

AM I AN ENTREPRENEUR/LEADER?

Businesses fail, and often. If you think you want to run your own business, but are not sure you can be a successful Entrepreneur, I am glad you are thinking about it... keep reading. How does an Entrepreneur think, act, and respond? Is your personality a fit for being a successful Entrepreneur? Do you have what it takes?

Until recently, Entrepreneurs were not well thought of. As recent as the 80's we looked on them as un-educated businessmen involved in shady dealings. There was a general lack of knowledge and information about what makes them successful.

Big business was the place to be, now that's all changed. Our generation and the ones after us expect so much more from our career/work than our parents did. We want money, satisfaction, self-expression and flexible hours such as a 4 day work week and telecommuting. We have more small businesses than ever before in our U.S. history. Besides, smaller businesses are now attracting great employees and competing with the corporate world by offering those employees exactly what they want.

Today we have books, courses and business coaches in abundance. Some universities now offer courses and degrees in entrepreneurship. Business professionals have vast resources and as a whole, we have learned a lot about what it takes to become a successful entrepreneur. I realize there is probably no such thing as the perfect entrepreneurial profile, I have noticed that there are many characteristics that seem to show up repeatedly in my work as a business coach. So from my work with hundreds of entrepreneurs as a coach and trainer, this is my summary.

Successful Entrepreneurs are, have or do

Available- In small businesses, where there is no depth of management, the owner must be present to win. They can't afford a support staff to cover all business roles and therefore need to either work long hours; have very talented people or both.

Self-Motivated-Entrepreneurs/leaders do not function well in structured organizations and do not like someone having authority over them. Rules, bureaucracy, and politics frustrate them. This is often what leads them to start their own business. They enjoy creating business strategies and thrive on the process of achieving their goals. Once they obtain a goal, they □uickly move to a greater goal. They constantly look to the future vision of the business. They have a compelling drive to do their own thing in their own way. They value freedom over money.

Well- Being- Successful Entrepreneurs are physically sound and in good health. They can work for extended periods as needed. They understand the relationship between a healthy body and a sharp mind.

Practical-Pragmatic- Entrepreneurs can accept what is and what is not and deal with issues accordingly. They may or may not be idealistic, but they are rarely unrealistic. They want to know the facts and conditions of a given situation at all times. They may be too trusting (because they are often idealists) and may not be sufficiently skeptical in their business dealings with other people.

Embrace Ambiguity – Entrepreneurs/leaders identify problems and begin working on their solution faster than other people. Uncertainty does not bother them because their Healthy Ego feels challenged and likes to solve problems. They are the natural "go-to" person in the group or business.

Intelligence - Successful Entrepreneurs/leaders think fast on their feet. They can comprehend complex problems and circumstances that may require planning, strategy, or working on multiple business ideas at once. They have a vision and are aware of important factors to consider. They are open-minded and will consider different perspectives. They seem flexible and are not afraid to change direction when failing.

Healthy Ego- Entrepreneurs/leaders are confident when they feel in control of what they're doing and often like to work alone. They tackle problems head-on and quickly with confidence. They are persistent in problem-solving and are not afraid of smart risks. They do well with adversity because they thrive on their own level of confidence. Someone saying or thinking they can't pull it off doesn't bother them at all.

Urgency- Entrepreneurs/leaders have a sense of urgency. They have the drive and high energy levels, they are achievement-oriented, and they are tireless in the pursuit of their goals. Idleness makes them impatient, on edge, and anxious. They thrive on activity and are not likely to be found at the nail salon or golf course. When they are in the entrepreneurial mode, they are more likely to be found getting things done instead of all the other "to-do's".

Emotional Stability- Successful Entrepreneurs/leaders can handle stress and are even having fun! They are challenged rather than discouraged by setbacks or failures. Entrepreneurs are surprisingly uncomfortable when things are going well. This is when they will probably find a new project on which to focus their creative energy.

Ability to let go-Entrepreneurs/leaders are not always the best "people" people. They are often impatient and drive themselves and everyone around them. They also resist delegating key decisions or responsibilities. My favorite coaching question for the Entrepreneur is "who can help you with this?" It shakes them up every time. It is not uncommon for the Entrepreneur to do the books, drive business development and buy the office supplies.

As the business grows and becomes an organization, Entrepreneurs/leaders go through a classic crisis (this is usually when they call us). They have become the bottleneck; their want for control has made it hard for them to hand over authority in the way that a growing business demands. Their strong direct approach makes them more likely to seek information directly from the source, bypassing the structured chains of authority and responsibility. Their interpersonal skills, which were adequate during the start-up phase, will cause them problems as they try to adjust and free themselves from the day to day operations. Cash flow, retention, and low morale are symptoms of this issue.

Do you recognize yourself? Did you locate your likely strengths as an Entrepreneur? Did you identify potential barriers to your success? Awareness matters here. Focus on your strengths, be aware of your weaknesses and go for it!

HUMAN RESOURCES - THE TALENT INTELLIGENCE OF BALANCED DECISION –MAKING

An everyday human being makes decisions from what food to eat, what clothes to wear, what route to travel and what actions to take in their respective roles. These roles may be:

Parent

Caregiver

Friend

Spouse

Employee

Entrepreneur

Manager

Executive

The results of their thought processes affect not only themselves but within the workplace others as well. This can be a serious concern especially for organizations that are looking to maximize their limited resources while creating a culture of high performance.

Regardless of the role, having the talent intelligence of balanced decision making can either enhance or diminish the individual's performance. For example, to decide using only emotions may cause logic to suffering and this may result in those all too familiar OOP$. Yes, there is a dollar sign after OOP$ because OOPS always costs dollars.

Defining this talent intelligence is fairly straightforward. This is the ability or capacity to be without bias (objective) and to be eＵuitable in the evaluation process specific to the different aspects within any given situation. Additionally, there also is the ability to maintain an inner balance between self-serving needs (oneself), the needs of others and the company or organization all simultaneously. Each of these aspects receives equal importance without favoring one or the other and this implies a strong positive code of ethics must be present.

When an individual demonstrates a high ability for this talent of balanced decision making, he or she does not favor one aspect over another. They approach their thought process by placing eＵual emphasis on all aspects resulting in a solution that is more than likely to please all involved.

On the flip side, those who lack this talent are just the opposite. They may overvalue one aspect such as themselves or a special interest group as they considered all factors. Their solutions may please a few people, but many leave many unhappy and discontented.

The behaviors for this specific talent may include some of the following:

Listening (actively) to all input from all vested parties

Conducting a cost and benefit analysis along with showing the results

Researching or investigating and providing accurate facts before making a decision

Keeping as much emotion out of the decision-making process as much as possible while still respecting intuitive thinking (instinct or gut)

For this talent of balanced decision making to be leveraged is one where expectations are clearly articulated. Employees must know the impact of their solutions and still feel the culture is open enough to accept possibly decisions that may be contrary to past ones.

One of the greatest challenges is this often heard remark: We never have done it that way. This comment may indicate that the original solution was never balanced by looking at all aspects, but may have been constructed with bias. For organizations to truly maintain their competitive position does re□uire this talent intelligence and for the executive team as well as the human resource department to understand how to support it especially during challenging times.

THE CHARACTERISTICS OF SUCCESSFUL ENTREPRENEURS/LEADERS

Entrepreneurs/leaders live in the future. They have creative personalities, are innovative, and thrive on change. But what makes an entrepreneur/leader successful? A good deal is known about what is required to be a successful entrepreneur/leader. An overriding factor found in most successful entrepreneurs is a tremendous need to achieve. The attitude seems to have everything to do with success in business, while factors such as intelligence, education, and personality are less significant.

The following attributes listed below are important characteristics of successful entrepreneurs.

An overpowering need to achieve, control, and direct

Usually, this is measured by the individual's internal ruler. They prefer environments where they have maximum authority and responsibility and do not work well in traditionally structured organizations. This is not about power, though. Entrepreneurs need to create and achieve by having control over events.

Good Health

Successful entrepreneurs/leaders must work long hours for extended periods. When they get sick, they recover quickly.

Self Confidence

Findings showed that as long as entrepreneurs were in control, they were relentless in pursuit of their goals. If they lost control, they quickly lost interest in the undertaking.

Comprehensive Awareness

They have a comprehensive awareness of a total situation and are aware of all the ramifications involved in a decision.

Realistic Outlook

There is a constant need to know the status of things. They may or may not be idealistic, but they are honest and straightforward and expect others to be the same.

Conceptual Ability

They have superior conceptual abilities. This helps entrepreneurs identify relationships in complex situations.

Low Need for Status

Their need for status is met through achievement, not through material possessions.

Objective Approach

An important trait is the ability to accurately weigh and measure risks in a sphere of realism. They take an objective approach to personal relationships and are more concerned with the performance and accomplishment of others than with feelings. They keep their distance psychologically and concentrate on the effectiveness of Operations.

Emotional Stability

They have the stability to handle stress from business and personal areas in their lives. Setbacks are seen as challenges and do not discourage them.

Attraction to Challenges

They are attracted to challenges but not to risks. It may look like they are taking high risks, but in actuality, they have assessed the risks thoroughly.

Describing with Numbers

They can describe situations with numbers. They understand their financial position and can tell at any time how much they have in receivables and how much they owe.

Follow-through

Meeting commitments and not quitting define this characteristic.

Positive mental attitude

Exhibiting confidence and believing in one's ability help the entrepreneur succeed.

A respectful attitude toward money

Money is not sought as an end in itself, but rather as a method of keeping score or as a tool toward accomplishments.

The tendency to anticipate developments

Making things happen, rather than reacting to outside developments, defines the entrepreneur's methods.

Resourcefulness

Successful people can handle unique problems in unique ways.

Communication abilities

These skills cannot be overstressed. Successful people have worked at developing the ability to communicate clearly and effectively.

Technical Knowledge

Sound working knowledge of both general business practices and the processes used to deliver goods and services is a must.

In conclusion, successful entrepreneurs will possess many of the attributes listed to be successful in their business of choice. Besides, one of the most important aspects of being a successful entrepreneur is to be involved in a business that you enjoy and many of the characteristics needed to be successful will come naturally.

LEARN THE TRUE SPIRIT OF AN ENTREPRENEUR

Do you aspire to become a successful entrepreneur? A lot of people nurse the same desire but not everyone can accomplish it for various reasons. There is a lot to learn in the world of business and so you should be willing to explore the different options to understand the right ways in which you can excel in your project.

You must have an undying passion and verve to excel in the project. If you do not fight to accomplish your goals, despite numerous challenges and setbacks, you will find it difficult to become an accomplished entrepreneur. The spirit of the entrepreneur is such that you are always ready and willing to take up the different challenges entrepreneurship ultimately presents.

As an entrepreneur, you are sure to meet a lot of different hurdles because the world of business is full of ups and downs. You cannot expect the journey to be smooth as there will always be moments that seem unbearable and these are the acid test. However, if you possess the spirit of the entrepreneur, it will guide you in such circumstances and provide you with the determination required to see you through the bad times.

No man can excel in the world of business without a resolve to find success. Along with a firm will and determination, there are responsibilities of an entrepreneur too. As an owner of the firm, you are responsible for the workers you have, the type of policy you follow, the way you help the society, the good and bad decisions you make as well as a whole host of other such responsibilities.

It is not easy to become a successful entrepreneur because you need to hone a lot of different skills. You must have leadership quality because as an entrepreneur, you need to lead from the front. Once you have managed to do so, you would be setting a good example for your crew to follow. This is an example of inspirational leadership.

Further, you need to work on your communication skills as well because it will help you in distributing the information in the right channels which will serve your purpose as well. You must be willing to socialize and make connections because when you do so your business will undoubtedly continue to prosper and grow.

Learn about the different responsibilities of an entrepreneur and then work upon them so that you can excel in your duties and become an example of a true leader. There are a lot of entrepreneurs who had a rough start in their businesses but the confidence and the zeal to succeed have brought them far. This is relentless persistence underpins what is meant by the spirit of the entrepreneur. So, do not lose hope and make sure to keep walking ahead because walking away from your dreams is never a solution.

4 HABITS OF SUCCESSFUL ENTREPRENEURS/LEADERS

Habits get a bum rap. When you think about your habits, I bet you think of the "bad" ones - the ones that you aren't particularly proud of, like eating too much sugar, or smoking, or dwelling on your negative thoughts. According to Webster's dictionary, a habit simply is A pattern or action that is ac□uired and has become so automatic that it is difficult to break.

It's easy to see how if you start a behavior, and continue to reinforce it, it quickly becomes a habit. The pint of Ben and Jerry's after dinner, playing Free Cell when you should be making calls, or always leaping to a negative conclusion when something happens. Once habits are formed, they can be hard to break, correct?

Get ready for a new perspective - habits can be good! What if, instead of relating to your habit as a problem, you were able to use your habits creatively to help you be more successful? Since habits are a natural part of our human experience (for better or worse), learning to capitalize on your innate ability to form positive patterns can mean a very successful life and business.

Here are 4 habits that successful entrepreneurs/leaders can learn to develop.

1. Build resilience. You don't need me to tell you - part of what goes with the territory when you're self-employed is incessant up and down of sales and cash flow. This is probably the number one stress producer for entrepreneurs.

Building the habit of resilience will help you to elegantly weather the unavoidable ups and downs. You build resilience by building your reserves. Some examples of reserves are cash (having 6-9 months of savings in the bank), self-esteem (plenty of positive regard for yourself) or confidence (feeling like an expert in your field).

What creates the most worry for you when faced with a stressor in your business? Focus on building a reserve of whatever will counter your number one stressor.

2. Become a passion junkie. Passion is an emotion - it's a feeling of excitement and intensity. It arises when you recognize something that authentically resounds in your being, and is a result of love and affinity. You know when you feel it and you know when it's missing.

Unfortunately, many people have developed the default habit of connecting with the emotion of fear instead. Fear (unless a polar bear is chasing you) fuels negative thinking and always results in stress. How do you connect with your passion? How can you begin to dis□ualify the fear-based thoughts that want to hog the road (of your mind)? Once you discover your passion, or remember it, taking active steps to stay connected to it will begin a new practice and encourage the passion habit in your life. 3. Be authentic. According to a psychologist, Abraham Maslow, "Authenticity is the reduction of phoniness toward the zero points." Strive to be honest in your personal and professional dealings so your behavior and speech are a true and spontaneous expression of your inner self. Live in a way that expresses your real vision, values, and characteristics.

Do you know who you truly are? By knowing yourself first, you will develop the habit of authenticity. What you put into the world will begin to be congruent with what you receive back from the world.

3. Work smarter not harder. If you're not careful, working hard can deteriorate into an exhausting habit, rather than an expression of an ethic. Often what drives and motivates entrepreneurs is the desire for success, but the pursuit of success often comes with mental baggage that can undermine it.

What are the mental "tapes" that cycle through your thought stream to undermine you? "I've got to work hard and prove myself"; "If I don't do it myself, it won't get done" or perhaps, "If I could just put in more time, I'd get it all done". Begin to build the habit of working smarter not harder. Counter the disempowering messages with some practical actions that put your business more on autopilot. Improve your systems, take the time to plan, and delegate.

4. Practice generosity. The international business networking organization BNI's motto is "Givers Gain". The premise is - more will come back to you if you focus on generously giving to your business network and your customers.

Giving, providing value, or offering superlative customer service is an attractive attribute and positive habit to develop. Tim Sanders, author of "Love Is The Killer App" articulates this business idea as, "the act of intelligently and sensibly sharing your intangibles with your business partners". This value can drive your business and your life up as far as you want it to go. What intangibles do you have to offer your world? What shift in your success and happiness do you see possible by focusing on giving rather than gaining?

If creating a habit is as easy as starting a behavior, and then repeating it (practice), consider the positive and powerful habits you could begin to form in your life and business, starting today! Going back to Webster's definition, a positive habit would be equally hard to break. Wouldn't that be nice for a change?

It's YOUR life... live it completely!

CONCLUSIONS

Positive entrepreneurial ability is closely related to the emotional state of an individual. High emotional intelligence provides for strong leadership skills and decision-making ability. A home-based business owner must be equipped to handle conflicting situations with a calm clear mind.

Emotional Perception:

Professional expertise and knowledge should be employed logically and sensibly to solve business problems. Successful business owners work to go beyond observing entrepreneurial activities as a mechanical function.

Entrepreneurs must have the ability to acknowledge and interpret personal emotions experienced to understand that of others. There should be cognizance of the power of emotions with professional and private actions carried out by an individual.

Business owners should have sound control over their emotions and have sensitivity along with empathy to that of others. Proprietors of a home-based business must be aware of their strengths and weakness to work towards beneficial emotional knowledge.

This enables the establishment of a personal connection with employees and co-workers that promotes productivity. Emotional intelligence works as a business asset increasing performance and your bottom line.

Conflict Resolution Skills and Sensitivity:

A self-confident and sensitive demeanor can help find mutually beneficial solutions with suppliers for product development. An amicable resolution can lower the risk of poor relations in the future.

Self-confidence and high emotional intelligence can help maintain a balanced temperament under difficult market conditions. The ability to listen to opinions and different points of view can help arrive at the right conclusion.

Humble Personality Traits:

A home-based business owner must be able to deal with clients and customers from varying social backgrounds. A sense of humility can help treat a potential customer with high respect and value.

Successful entrepreneurs do not employ an authoritarian relationship with their co-workers for strong productivity. There should be the presence of an understanding attitude for interactions with clients and employees.

Established business owners understand the importance of providing value to an employee in an organization for growth. Stressful circumstances like varying economic conditions and market ambiguity must be seen as an opportunity for development.

Acting on Positive Attributes:

There should be constant effort to further accentuate the existent key strengths of an individual for influential leadership. Established managers have a strong understanding of the human element at work in a business environment.

Home-based business owners must have the ability to take a risk and follow through on entrepreneurial ideas. There should be a shift in attention towards essential requirements over existent deficiencies.

By the way...do you want to learn exactly how to eliminate the high failure rate in a home business?

BIOGRAPHY

Derek Goneke has lived an extraordinary life, calls the great state of Tennessee home. Derek has always strived to be more, to be better, and to make an impact on the lives of others. He earned a Masters of Business Administration and has worked over a decade as an account executive for a Fortune 500 company. His dedication to his craft has earned him numerous awards in his field and propelled him around the globe in exploration. Derek's mind is constantly at work. He has become an entrepreneur and an author. He takes his experiences in business and as a father to craft entrepreneurship and children's books.

Derek's greatest passion- aside from being a self-proclaimed die-hard Liverpool FC fan- is being a father. Not only does this allow him to become a better man, it makes his books more appealing to children.

When he is not busy writing or managing high level accounts, Derek enjoys a quiet evening playing chess ,reading and spending time with family and friends.

If you could close your eyes and dream for a minute. Imagine a life where you are in total control of your time and your paycheck? where you are not trading Time for Money. How would that change your life, your family and legacy. This is what you get as an Entrepreneur, your sweat equals your rewards not the boss's check or the owner's profits. Does this sound like you a journey you want to take, the same journey your boss took to start the company you work for? Now you have the chance to be like your owner and do it on your own terms and time. I did and now i am loving it. I can promise you it was not easy it but very worthy. Stop wasting time that you can't get back by punching someone else's clock when you can create your own clock for others to punch and follow. The time is Now, for time waits for no one. Be like Nike and " JUST DO IT"

https://amzn.to/33cwZ9T